Was it for Real?

AKANSHA SINGH NAHAR

BlueRose ONE .com
Stories Matter
NewDelhi • London

BLUEROSE PUBLISHERS
India | U.K.

For permissions requests or inquiries regarding this publication, please contact:

BLUEROSE PUBLISHERS
www.BlueRoseONE.com
info@bluerosepublishers.com
+91 8882 898 898
+4407342408967

ISBN: 978-93-7139-366-9

Cover Design: Aman Sharma
Typesetting: Pooja Sharma

First Edition: August 2025

About the Author

Akansha Singh Nahar is an intuitive tarot reader and a passionate writer whose words mirror depth, healing, emotions, longing, and resilience.

She holds a diploma in ITI Fitter and a bachelor's degree in English Literature (Hons) from Bundelkhand University, Jhansi.

Was it for Real? is her debut poetry collection. Her work resonates deeply with those who loved fiercely, broke quietly, and grew in the shadows.

If her words found a home in your heart, you can write to her on Instagram:

*@aakanshaasinghh_*

About the Book

Was it for Real? is a short collection of poems, the quiet aftermath of heartbreak, wrapped in ink.

This book is for everyone who loved too deeply and were never loved enough.

Each poem is a wound.

Each word is a scream.

A question whispered in the dark.

Was it even real? or just for show?

- *silence*
- *scars*
- *survival*
- *self worth*
- *strength*

1-

You never said goodbye.
So I carved a thousand questions
on my ribcage
hoping your silence
might echo the answers.

2-

I do not cry for you anymore,
But some nights, silence tastes like rust.
The echoes of love long decayed,
Still whispers secrets in the dust.

I have been alone long enough,
To recall my shadow by its name,
To let the ache sit besides me,
Without asking why it came.

There is no thread left to unravel,
No wound still raw beneath my skin,
But something hollow hums within me,
A quiet ache that won't give in.

I have grown, I have healed,
Stitched my soul with careful hands,
Still some ghosts refuse to leave,
They linger where the daylight bends.

3-

His touch was like a feather,
softly having an essence over me
Fingers cold as an ice,
Like a tip of water on a petal,
Eyes closed
Hallucinating like under an influence of a psychedelic drug
Breath trembling, lips shivering,
A moment in the time lingering,
A moment so vivid, like a blur in the wind.

4-

I wonder,
How your hands never tremble,
While touching someone else
When you're the one who said,
"You're mine".
Did you ever mean it,
Or;
Was I just someone you held
Without feelings?

5-

Music blasting, windows down,
The car hummed a song only we could hear,
The night air wrapped around us like a
whisper
Cold breeze singing a melody,
Only for our ears.

Bodies swayed away with the music beats,
The car pacing in sync with our racing hearts,
The road to home never felt so dreamy,
Only to make me realise someday,
I would have to return lonely.

6-

Then one day,
No explanation, no goodbye,
How could you just leave me like that?
You didn't slam the door,
You let it creak, Slowly shut,
While I stood there,
Still waiting,
For the version of you
Who never really tried.

7-

There was a time,
I folded myself small,
Just to fit inside the hollow space,
He carved for me.

A time when his words,
Cut deeper than knives,
When his laughter felt like a noose,
Tightening around my throat.

8-

They mocked me,
The ones he called his friends,
They spat my name like venom,
And he never once,
Wiped the poison away,

9-

Then,
He touched another,
And another,
And another,
And another,
Until the love I bled for him,
Was nothing,
But a stain;
On his careless hands.

10-

I will never forget,
The way you never thought,
I was worthy,
Not of your time,
Not of your truth,
Not even a gentle goodbye.

11-

The city carried our love in its heart,
The passing streets, the red lights,
Road to our homes,
Where we never wanted to reach.

Car windows fogged with hurried kisses,
One more, one more,
Before I leave for home.

The places we used to eat,
Still echoes the stories we never finished.

The city knows your name,
I still wonder if it was all a dream,
The city is suffocating,
Living here feels exhausting.

12-

I think, I know,
He never liked me,
He liked the idea,
The idea of me,
The way I stayed,
Even when it hurt,
The way I loved,
And cared,
Even when he made me feel worthless,

But me? Never!
He never touched the parts,
That screamed the loudest.

13-

There were nights,
I cried like a child,
Not for a toy,
But for someone,
Who promised they would stay.

I wept,
For the kind of love,
I thought I deserved,
But never received,
And no one saw me,
Not even you.

14-

I kept standing there,

Weeping,

Crying,

Shivering,

At the thought of you,

With someone else.

And you?

You walked away,

Smiling with her, Leaving me in pieces,

I still haven't found.

15-

You gave me the trauma,
The trauma of humiliation,
Of abandonment,
Of watching your hands,
Find comfort on someone else's skin
The trauma of imagining you,
Unzipping yourself for strangers,
While I stayed clothed,
In memories.

16-

sometimes, I wonder,
If you ever remember me?
Not as the girl you left,
But as the girl,
Who loved you,
When you didn't deserve.

17-

Do you ever feel guilt?
When you laugh now,
Do my tears echo somewhere?
In your chest.
Do your hands remember the warmth I gave them?
Do you remember the heartlessness you left behind?
In a girl, who waited too long,
For love,
You never meant.

18-

I still remember the shirt you wore,
The day you first held my hand,
The cologne you used,
The one I still can't bear to smell,
I remember your laugh,
And how it faded over time,
I remember the look in your eyes,
When you stopped loving me,

It's cruel,
How I remember everything,
But you've forgotten me,
When I've already existed in your life.

19-

Why did you do this to me?
I asked the mirror,
The pillow,
The night sky,
Again and again.

But silence,
Was the only one,
Who ever answered .

20-

It was 2 am,
My room was quiet,
But inside me,
A storm raged.
I was crying like I would die,
Choking on sobs,
That refused to leave gently.
I curled into myself,
Clawing for Breath,
As if grief had hands,
Around my throat.

No one knew, no one came,
Only the night watched, as I shattered quietly.

21-

I wonder if I ever cross your mind,
I wonder if you ever,
Cried for me,
Like I did for you,
Unseen,
Unloved,
Unheard.

22-

Did you bury me?
Somewhere in silence;
Where even guilt,
Refuse to grow.

23-

The tears dried,
But the ache didn't leave.
It just sat there,
Like dust on everything,
I touched.
I smiled at the world.
But inside me,
Grief made a home.

24-

Do you ever remember
That long drives under the quiet sky?
That laughter we shared
When your friends made me feel like I belonged?
Do you ever go back?
To those nights we didn't speak much,
But the silence felt warm
Because we were on call

Or did you forget it all?

25-

But why did they hate me (your friends)?
They didn't even know me,
But they carried knives
Etched with my name.
Their laughter,
A quiet war against my presence,
Their eyes, always searching for flaws
I never meant to show.

26-

I walked in with love,
Bare hands, open heart,
And still
They called me too much, too soft,
Too loud even in my silence,

Was loving you?
A crime enough?
To be hated by those,
Who stood beside you?

What did they whisper to you?
When I wasn't there.
And why?
Why did you listen?

27-

I kept asking myself
Was I too much,
Or,
Never enough?

Did I love you wrong?
Or did you just want to leave?

Was there a moment, you looked at me
And decided you were done?

Where did I go wrong?
Where did I go wrong?
Where did I go wrong?

Even now,
I search for answers.

28-

You made me stop believing in softness,

In forever, in love,

You say I'm cold now.

But love,

You lit the fire,

And left me in.

29-

You say,

I have changed, I have become distant,

I'm no longer soft.

But;

You don't talk about,

The nights you made me cry,

The parts of me you crushed,

The love you walked over,

It's been 2 years now,

And I'm still stitching,

The pieces you broke.

Of course! I changed.

You killed the version, the happy me,

The one who loved you.

30-

Each time I came back,
You opened the door,
With the same smile,
The same warmth,
As if you never broke me.
No apology, no trace of guilt,
Just your voice, treating me like a passing thought,
Not a bleeding memory.

31-

Why did you never return?

Why did you never apologize?

Why did I stay shattered?

While you moved like nothing happened.

32-

I lost my heart,
But never got yours,
I lost myself but never found you,
Even when you were beside me,
I gave it all
And you,
You just took.

33-

I forgot you,
The voice, the laugh,
Even the birthday
But this heart, it still flinches,
At songs we danced to,
Streets we walked.
I forgot you,
But this heart,
Keeps searching in crowds,
For a face,
I swore I let go.

34-

I didn't plan to take you name,
Not today,
Not in this story,
Not even once,
But somehow,
Your shadow crawled between the lines,
Your voice echoed in a stranger's sentence,
Your memory sat quietly, beside my sigh,

I swear!
You weren't supposed to show up,
And yet,
You always do.

35-

Yet,

Not sorrow, not longing,

Not love, not hate,

Just something weightless, nameless,

Just silence, loud enough,

To tear through,

Everything I ever believed in.

36-

Even after everything you put me through,

The disrespect,

The silence,

The humiliation,

The betrayal,

I came back!

I came back,

With trembling hope clinging to that one thought,

Maybe now,

Maybe now;

You will value me.

37-

How foolish of me!
To think love could fix what hurt me,
I believe that I stayed long enough,
Loving enough,
You would finally see me.

How foolish of me!
To return after every storm,
Still soaked,
Still shivering,
Still hoping;

How foolish of me,
To carry a heart that bled for you!
But maybe,
I wasn't foolish;
It was my love in it's rarest form.

38-

You never said sorry,
And I no longer need you to,

I forgave you!
Not because you deserved it
But;
Because my soul
Deserved rest.

39-

Yet;
Some days the memory stings,
Like cold winds,
Other days;
The memory sits like a,
Silent guest,
Something familiar,
Now, I sit with it, as long as I can,
Before it leaves again.

40-

My rage was silent
For a long time it didn't scream,
It sat quietly between clenched teeth
And teary pillows,
Taking notes of every tear I shed
And;
Every time I was blamed for loving too much.

I watched you laugh,
While I was biting down on all the things,
I should've said.

41-

You lit the match and

I, I burned myself,

And then;

I blazed,

I composed poetries with the ashes,

You thought you would ruin me,

But;

You made me indestructible.

42-

How foolish of me!
To beg for love,
From the hands,
That only knew,
How to break me.

43-

I lowered my worth,
Like a price tag,
Hoping you'd pick me
Just once,
I bent my spine, into bridges,
You burned everytime,
You crossed.

I came back, after every betrayal,
Not once, not twice,
But every time,
You played with my heart,
And still;
I whispered,
Maybe this time....

44-

I forgave you,
For my chest,
To rise and fall,
Without heaviness,
I stitched peace,
Into the places you tear apart,
Planted softness,
Where your hands left bruises,
Closure never came in your words,
So;
I built it myself,
Quietly, painfully,
Like a girl
Buying her favorite flower,
In a garden,
That no longer blooms.

45-

My anger didn't shout,

It remembered,

And now;

It speaks in poems,

You will never read.

46-

She is not waiting at the door anymore,
She doesn't re read messages,
She doesn't shrink for anyone,
And;
Her eyes,
Don't cry anymore,
The tears dried.

47-

Maybe,

This was always the end.

Sometimes,

I wish it shouldn't have began,

But;

Maybe I was meant to love you,

Long enough,

Until I learn to love myself.

I no longer search for answers,

I no longer hold my breath.

I accept it now!

Some stories are meant to end,

Some people are meant to

Burn out quietly,

Without apologies,

Without closure,

And maybe

That's okay,

But;

Maybe.

48-

I won't say i deserved it,
But i think,
The pain was worth it,
I'm not grateful to you,
Never, ever.
But;
I'm grateful to the ache.

To;
The way my heart ached,
The way my eyes cried,
The way my hands shivered,
The way my voice choked,
The way my soul shattered,

I think something in me changed,
Something I can't explain,
I don't feel much now,
Perhaps,
I'm an emotionless person.
Perhaps,
The pain made me better
But;
Perhaps.

49-

The saddest part is,
I still don't hate you,
I just wish,
You had tried.

Tried to hold me,
To see me,
To choose me,
To love me....

50-

I hope you never feel it,
I hope you never cry,
The way I did.
I hope your hands,
Never tremble at 2 am,
With grief sharp enough,
To pierce your own skin.

I hope you never find yourself,
In the moments of pain,
That feels physical,
Even though you can't see it.

I wouldn't wish that kind of pain,
On,
Even the one,
who gave it to me.